MY BIG PICTURE DICTIONARY

Illustrated by
Peter Adby &
Alan Fredman

AWARD PUBLICATIONS
London

Related titles available

PICTURE DICTIONARY
MY ANIMAL ABC BOOK
MY ANIMAL COUNTING BOOK
MY FIRST PICTURE BOOK OF POETRY

ISBN 0-86163-129-3

Printed in Belgium

A a

acorn

alligator

anchor

apple

almond

arrow

apron

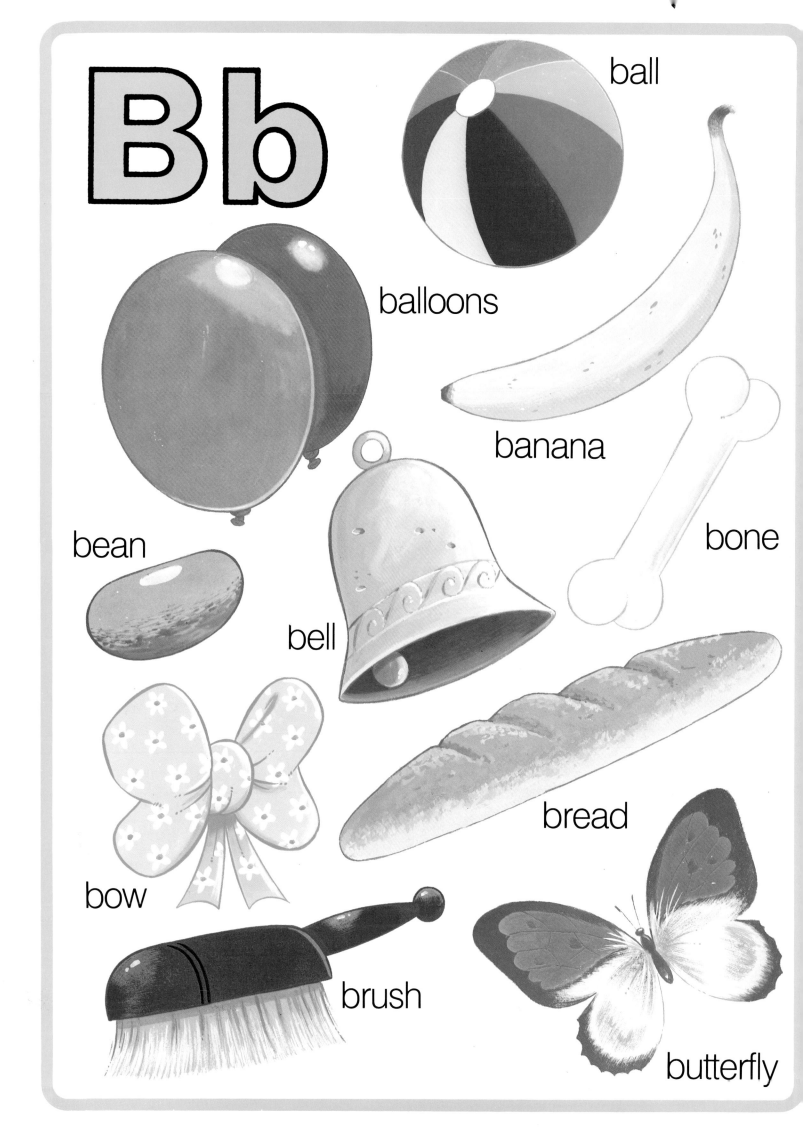

B b

ball

balloons

banana

bone

bean

bell

bow

bread

brush

butterfly

Cc

candles

cake

carrot

cat

clock

cactus

clown

cup

cushion

Dd

dart

desk

dishes

drum

doll

duck

dog

Ee

earth

egg

ear

eagle

eggcup

8
eight

elephant

envelope

eskimo

F f

face

feather

fish

flowers

fir

flute

frog

Gg

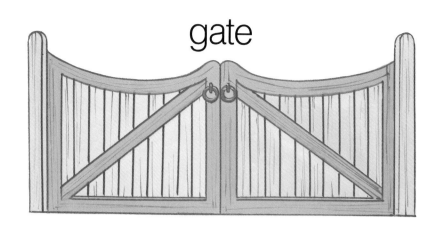
gate

girl

glass

gold

gorilla

gong

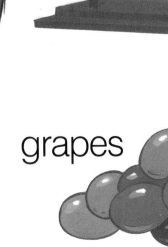
grapes

Hh

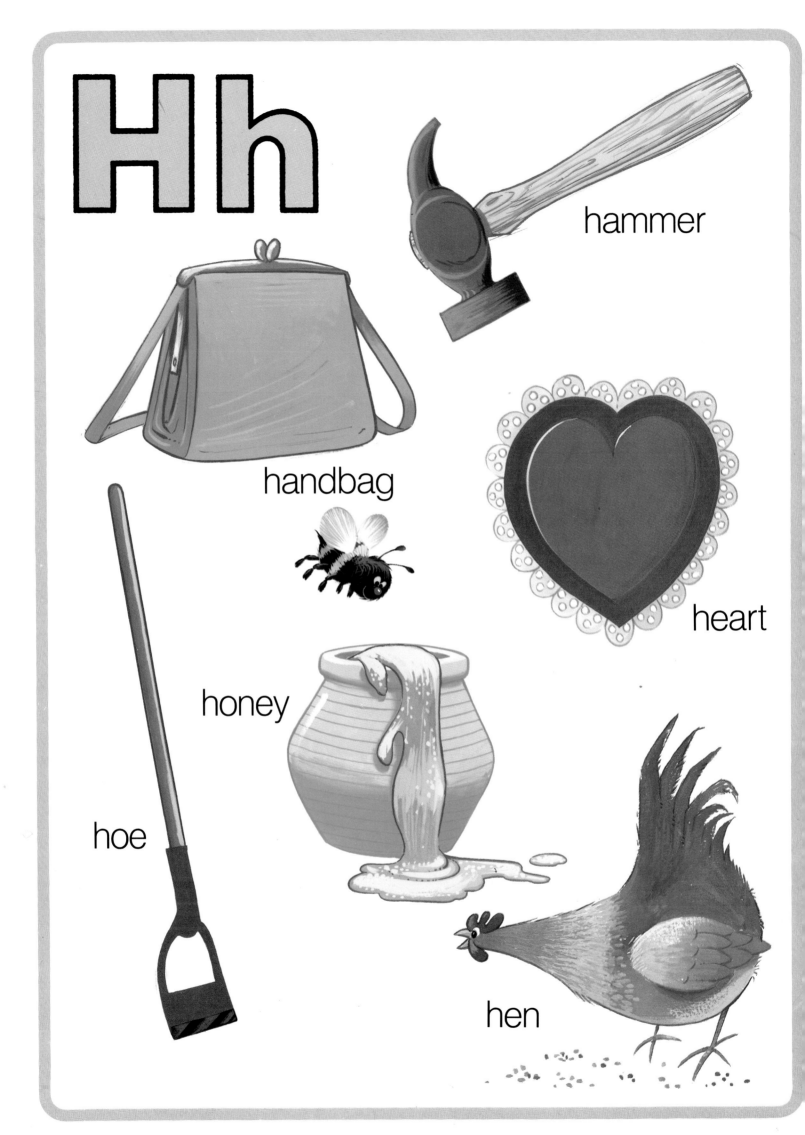

hammer

handbag

heart

honey

hoe

hen

Ii

icecream

igloo

indian

ivy

Jj

jewels

jug

jam

K k

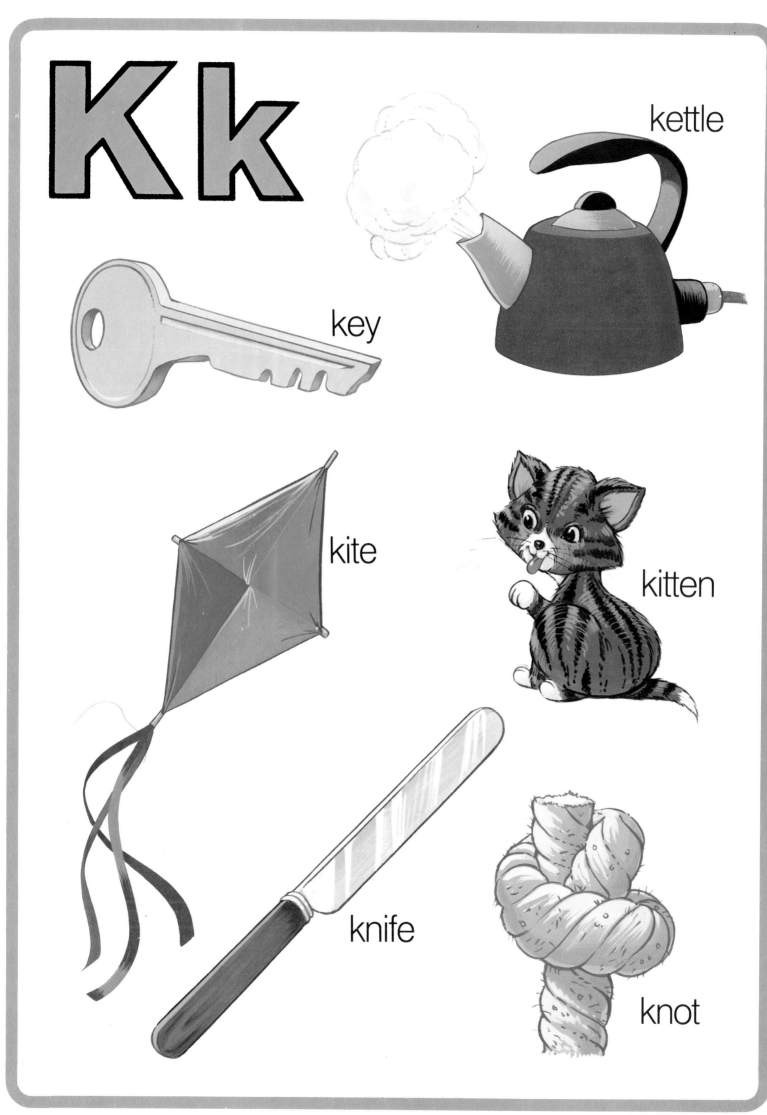

kettle

key

kite

kitten

knife

knot

Ll

lamb

leaf

leek

log

lemon

ladder

lobster

lollipops

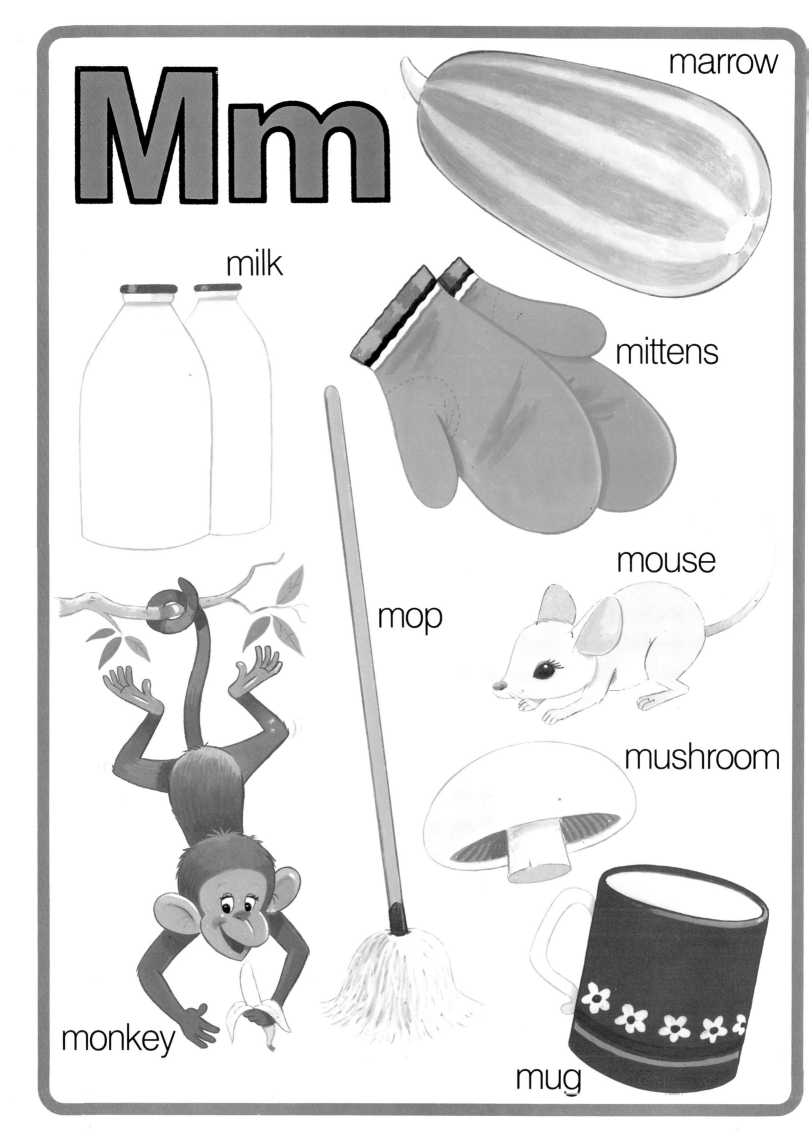

Mm

marrow

milk

mittens

mouse

mop

mushroom

monkey

mug

Nn

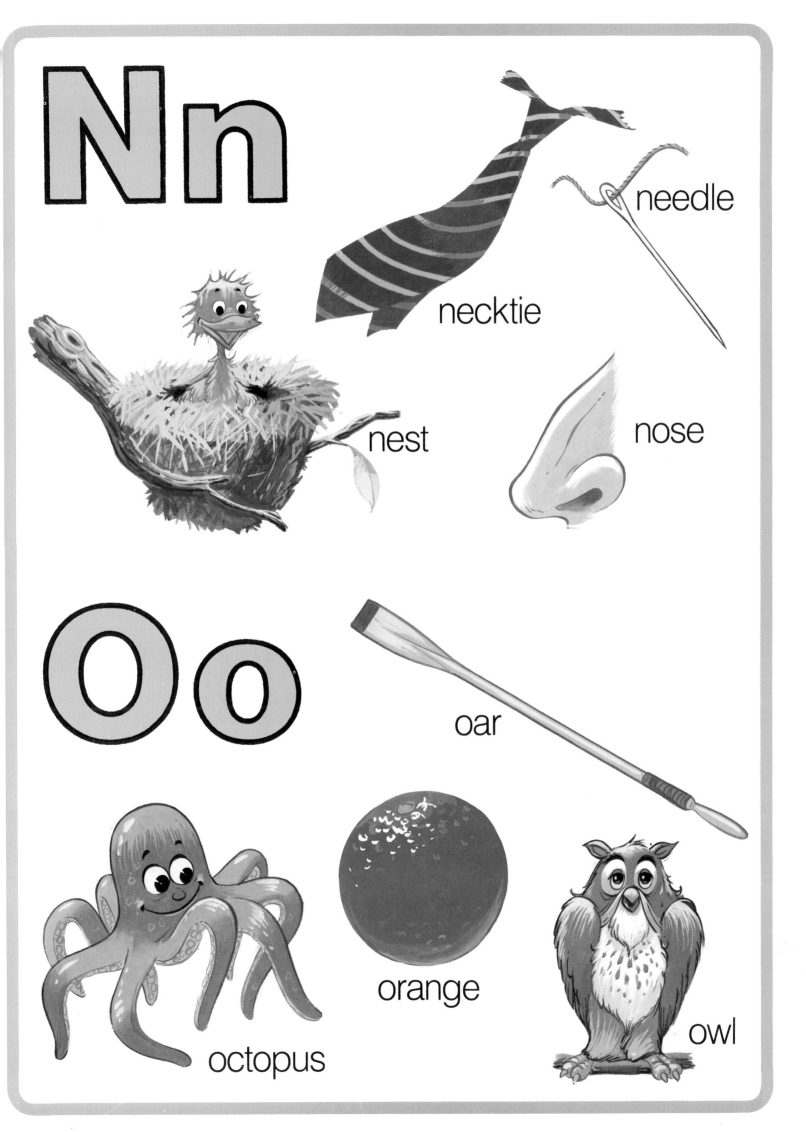

needle

necktie

nest

nose

Oo

oar

octopus

orange

owl

P p

paint
(pink)

paintbrush

parcel

penguin

pear

peas

peapod

pen

pencil

puppy

potatoes

Qq

queen

quill

quoits

quilt

Rr

radishes

robin

rose

Ss

spoon

slippers

squirrel

swan

Tt

teapot

tomato

tortoise

trumpet

U u

umbrella

unicorn

uniform

V v

vase

vulture

violin

W w

watch

whale

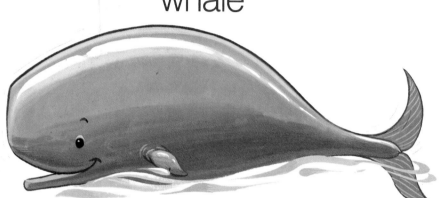

window

X x

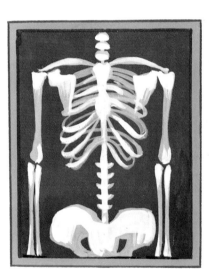

x-ray

xylophone